A Heartbeat Away

A HEARTBEAT AWAY

Finding hope after grief and loss

Flappy Lane Fox

The Child Bereavement Trust

The Child Bereavement Trust
Aston House, High Street, West Wycombe
Bucks, HP14 3AG

www.childbereavement.org.uk

First published 2005

© Flappy Lane Fox, 2005

A catalogue record for this book is
available from the British Library

ISBN 0 9521661-6 X

Printed and bound in Great Britain by
Creative Print & Design (Wales), Ebbw Vale

To my children, Harry and Lottie,
and to all bereaved families and friends

CONTENTS

FOREWORD

Birth and death are the certainties that embrace us all, regardless of our faith, race or culture. And while death at the end of a life lived well may, on reflection, be some cause of celebration, premature bereavement is universally shocking and the pain seemingly unbearable. When such tragedy strikes, our life grinds to a halt and a deep chasm opens up between ourselves and the world we once knew. But, although the pain never entirely goes away, it is possible in time to take our first steps towards a kind of acceptance and to re-establish links to our former life.

Before you read Flappy Lane Fox's story, you may already have some experience or understanding of the depth and duration of suffering that bereavement can cause. However, when you reflect on all the child-related tragedies that happen on a daily basis, varying in context and detail but all contributing to the sum total of human desperation, you may be surprised to learn that it is only in the last ten years that any form of service and support has been available to professionals, who are so often in the front line of tragedy.

The poems and extracts in this book, all written from harsh experience, chart the journey from grief, rage and anguish to the first kindling of a hope in the future. From this point, it may be possible for us to look back on our loved ones with love and gratitude, and then move on in a creative, caring and fulfilling way, nurturing them in our hearts for ever.

If in this book you find one line to comfort, strengthen and, above all, provide a modicum of peace and hope, then Flappy Lane Fox's efforts will have been worthwhile. I do hope that this book will reach all those in need of support and thereby benefit the continuing work of The Child Bereavement Trust: an inspirational charity that is there for all of us when we need it most.

His Royal Highness The Prince of Wales

PREFACE

❧

'… death eventually separates everyone from each other.
It is only the vividness of memory that keeps the dead
    alive forever.'

JOHN IRVING, *THE WORLD ACCORDING TO GARP*

In this book, Flappy Lane Fox draws together shared memories, experiences and learning through a collection of writings from many sources that will touch each of us in different ways. In sharing her feelings about the death of her son, Harry, Flappy demonstrates the uniqueness of grief and the importance of memories in helping us mourn. Memories can bring us comfort and support through enabling us to experience our joy, sorrow and pain. Memories are a recognition of what we have had; they belong to us and can never be taken from us.

The Child Bereavement Trust is a national UK charity working to improve the care and support offered to bereaved families. In helping us at The Child Bereavement Trust understand what really matters, grieving families have taught us the importance of listening, appreciating and accepting their feelings and experiences.

For Flappy, Harry's death was the beginning of a whole new changed way of life. Within the pages of this book, we hope you will find connection and meaning in your own unique experience of loss, and inspiration and encouragement as you move forward.

Julia Samuel   *Jenni Thomas OBE*   *Ann Chalmers*
Founder Patron   Founder and President   Chief Executive

Flappy's story

Before I begin, I would ask, is a mother's grief for the loss of her child a 'given' – so obvious an affliction that there needs be little explanation or justification for our subsequent erratic, insane behaviour; a wound so deep, no matter how many plasters are applied, it will never heal; a sentence of life imprisonment. Having joined this sorrowful club of forlorn imprisonment, I would like to explain, through my own experience, just how we club members cope, in the hope that this will help all those of you who are grieving, at whatever stage you are in your grieving.

The death – when time stands still

5 September, 1999 – approximately 11.00 am local time, mid-France. I am lying by a swimming pool alone, idly studying an army of ants dragging a dead fly to their lair, wondering how to resist a foie gras lunch, for which this region is famed, and generally relaxing as one might on holiday. I don't remember why my mobile telephone is in my bag, but its ring surprises me.

Peter, my ex-husband and father of our children, Harry ('H-bottom') and Lottie, is talking and something in his tone suggests unease. 'I have some bad news,' – perhaps my house has been burgled, or my car stolen – 'Harry had an accident last night and he has

DIED … DIED … DIED …' (this last word echoing on and on). 'Don't make such an obscene joke, have you lost your mind?' I think; anyway, I reason quite illogically, nothing possibly could have happened to Harry as Lottie is away in Australia. Not realizing how fast the split-second shock has set in, I repeat staccato my vehement disbelief over and over, reality totally suspended, only a small dull thud of fear quietly thumping.

The world is groaning to a halt, and yet the ants continue their relentless labour under sunny skies. My head is deafening – shrinking and expanding like an accordion playing hideously off-key a mishmash of rock metal – and after seemingly hours, but in reality perhaps minutes, the penny doesn't drop exactly, rather it teeters on the edge of the precipice as I hang on with bloodied fingernails. Peter's sister Jill was killed in a car crash, aged 22, when Peter was in Australia aged 25, and he and I acknowledge this macabre coincidence. Does this mean I have accepted Harry, my darling dearest son, has died. (I can still hardly type or say that word.)

Mother Nature, I think, took over the unenviable task and helped me tidy my belongings, put on a kikoy and, with ball-and-chain feet, walk back to the hotel room. There were no tears, screaming or even a hint of anguish on the short journey back, and although I felt as conspicuous as an alien, I gave no hint of it. I apologized to Martin (my partner and subsequent husband) for ruining his holiday – perhaps postponing the awful moment of truth – and for a few minutes more was able to pretend that it simply wasn't true, and even continued my watercolour painting of an enchanting hamlet high above the hotel.

Being so far away from the scene of death, gave time an inexplicable unreality, and I felt as if I was hovering above the Earth in a twilight zone – a vignette perhaps, a mirror image of how Harry was coping. They say the deceased travel for forty days and this was after all only day one. Would he have a map to hand?

That night, you see, at approximately 2.30 am. Harry had hit a tree, the only tree on that side of the road for one mile, swerving, I like to think, to avoid a fox, travelling over the speed limit and over the drink limit – neither overly so – keen to return to bed after a wonderful party. He had meant to stay the night and had been given a billet, but something drew him on – we all have choices. Three miles from Sherston, he died instantly from the impact of hitting the tree, his car careering out of control, flipping over and over and throwing him free. Quite shortly after, I dreamt of him stepping sprightly along that road smiling (before I knew the facts). Talking to Nats, my goddaughter and soulmate of H, we argued the toss as to whether H was with me in France or her in America – of course, he was with all of us who needed him – a very busy bloke indeed.

Returning by car to England, there was a succession of dire 'on another planet' calls. My main objective was to get to Heathrow Airport in order to meet Lottie's return flight from Australia. Darling Lottie had rung during her travelling gap year for a chat and was rewarded with the news of her brother's death; my heart bled and bled and bled for her, as I imagined how she took the news in a pub, surrounded by newfound back-packing friends. So instantly alone and uncomprehending, in a massive country with no one close to help share her plight, she would have to piece together her journey home to hell. Mel, my best friend and H's godmother, kept in constant touch from Canada, coercing an army of support as only she can do, gently guiding and advising during those two days of spaced-out driving. The extraordinarily few times I consciously thought of Harry were permanently of peace – since his favourite expression was 'peaceful'. I'm certain H-bottom was already transmitting strongly to me – RIP.

Peter and I met Lottie's flight – thereafter, for two long days the three of us stayed cocooned at home in London, cursing, crying, laughing, needing no one else, and only leaving each other for bare essentials. It was an awesome time of unity, born, I suppose, out of the many shared memories and ties that all families have, but don't necessarily appreciate in humdrum everyday life. I felt relieved, on Lottie's behalf, that, even though divorced, Pete and I were so united; we sat in crumpled heaps, perched on top or between piles of curtains and furniture, as my tiny house was in the turmoil of redecoration – somehow this topsy-turvy mess brought a certain comfort, as if sharing our inner chaos. I was strongly discouraged from seeing Harry's body, and so numbstruck was I that I went along with this. The horrendous niggling thought was conceived, but not admitted, that perhaps he was decapitated. Just to have seen his big toes would have been enough. It is my lifelong regret.

Some courageous friends crept through the door, bear-hugging, and offering to help with the daunting task of planning H's funeral and Thanksgiving. We humbly received the flowers, letters and food that poured in, including treats for our dog Bottom (a black Labrador beloved by all, called 'Wuffling' by Harry). In many ways, one could have been tricked into believing this was a celebration, with all the care and attention we received, and I thought often of the acute isolation of the thousands of solitary people out there, left to cope entirely alone when a loved one dies. Thank God there were the three of us to share our numb, shattering grief, and the tiny flashes of – dare I say it – fun, as we received the gifts.

The reactions

The harrowing grief and searing rawness of spirit remained firmly below the surface, as if anaesthetized and weighted down in the pit of my stomach – in fact, the anaesthetic remained virtually effective for 18 months. When seeing our friends' faces etched in sorrow, I had to pinch myself that it was for us they were grieving. I learnt very early that if someone touched unintentionally any one of the hundreds of raw nerves, bringing unstaunched feelings crawling upwards, the Oscar-winning ability to sidestep them was quite remarkable. It was a sure sign the anaesthetic was clearly working; I would deflect any unwelcome comment, put up barriers of Thames' proportions, change the conversation and make a joke. Yes – a joke. English stiff upper lip also worked well, and although tears came spasmodically, laughing was therapeutic. Humour after all is the thread that keeps us sane, and this was a warped sense of the ridiculous, enough to make any weirdo howl with laughter. In hindsight, I think I behaved normally, but the effort spent achieving this was vast – was I convincing anyone anyway, and if so for what purpose? Grief is permitted (they used to wear black armbands to advertise the case), so why was I keeping up false appearances? Or did I not want to admit to Harry's death, too frightened that if I 'let go' I would never regain sanity?

I yawned constantly, and yet could not sleep; I hugged myself imagining it was Harry's bear-like hug – such a brilliant hugger, often lifting me off my feet to stretch my backbone. I spent hours stultifyingly staring ahead into nothing – and then outrageous bursts of energy like never before, adrenalin pumping, I would contemplate climbing Everest. Was this normal? I had no answer, as I hadn't been there, done it or bought the t-shirt.

The variety of peoples' reactions was astounding; some in a brave and straightforward way expressed their grief, others lectured and divulged their own problems (probably never discussed or even addressed by them before); then there were those who, I'm sure, were just as gutted, but quite unable to cope with the mere mention of Harry's name. Perhaps this latter group were terrified to express anything for fear of getting it wrong or hurting us. Harry, however problematical at times, was a gift for the 24 years of his life, and that it would be an insult to his immensely kind and caring spirit to assume he had suddenly vanished. In fact, he is 'there' all the time, almost more so than before, and so to talk to him and about him is just the most normal, natural instinct, as one would do of any child sharing one's daily life. There is a balance to be found for a grieving person between having the door of communications slammed shut, and talking on obsessively for twenty-four hours a day. But, oh, how to reach the balance – I know I still want to hug anyone who mentions H-Bottom's name, I am so grateful for the acknowledgement.

Perhaps it is impossible to assess another's pain, but if we have been through a life-shattering experience, we are more able to imagine, empathize with, and understand that person's feelings, and realize the all-important art of listening. The loneliness of grief is unbearable, and although we are all alone, the minute the umbilical cord is cut, somehow this loneliness seems contagious, and we appear as lepers – definitely to be avoided. Giving time and listening are gifts to grieving people.

When eyes glazed over if I spoke of H for too long (read two minutes max), I felt so distressed, pitifully alone. I wrote earlier of bereavement being like joining an exclusive macabre club, with only those members knowing the rules and regulations. Certainly, the members that I have since met up with have been compassionate, sensitive and profoundly interested in all aspects of other's traumas, comparing notes, giving wise advice and intuitively helping. I now know, as never before, grief is 'better out than in'. We may need help to force it into the open; the alternative – imploding and living on 'shut down' – is not only a health hazard but also produces a bitter and isolated person.

Easier said than done, though. As I write, over five years, I still have a long journey ahead. The overpowering shock that careers round the corner, sometimes sweeps me off my feet: 'Harry Sidebottom dead, gone, not here any longer? Perhaps on holiday? No, dead, gone'. It is so horrendous, the disbelief still so astounding, it makes me ask if my brain is intact. Perhaps 99% of what passed for a brain is fragmented now, and lost forever in the muddle of my head. It would be easier to have a leg lopped off or an eye gouged out, because the affliction is so obvious, the recuperation and acceptance long and arduous maybe, but in the end 'sorted', rather than the incessant internal wound that never heals.

The humour

I think I need a little light relief: I am shattered having got this far in trying to explain. Being most impatient by nature, I want a miraculous cure this minute. By the way, do you think you can get married in heaven. I would so love Harry to have children, and me grandchildren – but weirdly he always said he would never have children, but perhaps he was only talking about earthly children.

Humour and a sense of the ridiculous is the microscopic thread that weaves through life, preventing us going into a madhouse, monastery, convent, or whatever. So many times I have been surprised to find myself doubled up with laughter, it's hard to believe. A measure of guilt always ensues, as if the right to mirth should forever be denied. However, I reason, anything that helps and a little bit of what you fancy is not a crime, is it? Don't panic I tell myself, Harry had a dry and very well-developed sense of humour, and it's probably him sending a little bit of light relief – anyway, he should be the guilty one, landing me in this shit. Also, half of me is still at school, and giggling is a seriously childish pastime: Harry's death may well become a lifelong excuse for anything – even a crocodile tear or two. At this point I am remembering some of the bizarre and hilarious situations that helped a little to lift the suffocation of my grief, dire black humour maybe, but I hope you'll smile with me.

- ❧ We have a walnut tree planted in H's honour, and the plaque beneath it is printed with the wrong dates. How could I do that?!

- I took H's ashes to the undertakers to have them put into boxes for Lottie and I – I went back to collect them and left one behind.
- Netia, a girlfriend of H's wrote a recipe book and asked me to contribute; I wrote Harry's Lemon Pots recipe, with the juice of one lemon. The only mistake that came back from the printers was Harry's Lemon Pots recipe, with the juice of eleven lemons! A poor friend, aptly named Squeeze, actually cooked and ate this recipe!
- Sitting in my car with the door open, feeling as depressed as a cat, suddenly a bird flew overhead and shat directly on my head.
- Sitting at dinner one evening, on my left was an old school friend of H, on my right a cousin of Martin who is a Coeliac. (Harry was a Coeliac for the first eight years of his life.)
- At H's inquest , a blinding flash of sunlight on an otherwise gloomy day, and Harry smiling intensely at me: 'Sorry Mum, to put you through this.'
- Having Reike one day, H appeared directly before me, smiling, and said, 'Do stop fussing mother, I'm fine.'

The funeral and thanksgiving

Our loved ones are only truly dead if they are forgotten. There was relatively little time to plan our tiny funeral, attended by Peter, Lottie and me, with Bottom guarding both us and Harry in his coffin. When I saw the coffin arrive, I was full of anxiety for it looked way too small, so putting on my decorator's hat I paced out the length checking it against Harry's six foot frame – how bizarre was that: just another way of avoiding dealing with the real issue? The service felt both a charming celebration and a vile ritual, conducted weirdly on a God-given sunny day, and us drawn as moths to the light, heavy hearts coated with thin smiles for those in the choir, the pall bearers and vicar. The first moment of deep down realization: my darling dearest son, whom I quite simply loved, confined to the claustrophobia of a beastly box, with only the tiniest ventilation, wearing something that we had not chosen (I should have thought of that), and without any question squashed head to toe in there – a chink in my armour beginning to appear, in as much as I think I accepted that his body was in there. Certainly, his spirit was soaring above the church, although at that point, numb in spirit myself, I only felt an inkling of this child of mine driving the three of us on.

In that small funeral service, not needing to entertain or put on a show, I calmly read 'Death is nothing at all', directed entirely to Peter and Lottie, feeling that it was actually H reading it – no obvious emotion, anaesthetised. We then had to deal with the crematorium, watch his body disappear behind crude curtains. In what seemed like an instant we were left with only a pot of ashes and a beautiful mass of white lilies. Thank you very much we all said – what else can you say? At this point, brain, spirit and soul were all on overload and a total blank arrived. I remember nothing at all for a while. In addition, perhaps it wasn't helped by the shock of returning to the house Peter and I created during 25 years of marriage – I don't know. I've always found, in moments of turmoil and desperation, that I can conjure up a wall to protect and help me deal with whatever – I often wonder if others do this. The punch line hits home sooner or later, though.

The Thanksgiving service fell to me to organize, with the unfailing support of a few very kind friends. With me going on my old friend Overload in a thrice, it was a miracle I got it sorted. Harry was delighted with the result I just know – it was simply stunning in every respect; when we arrived there was Nats, my gorgeous goddaughter and soulmate of Harry, spreadeagled against the church walls talking earnestly to H, preparing for her talk – somehow a certain peace prevailed. Bottom barked as the wonderful vicar and choir walked up the aisle – H saying hello perhaps. So many potions and pills were offered in order to 'up' us or 'down' us, but, strangely, none were needed as we proceeded with terrifying calm through our farewell to H. (I was gutted that my name was mentioned once only in the main address and thought a mother might deserve a smidgen more.)

During tea at Sherston after the service, the three of us 'managed' with the skill of consummate actors, only recoiling occasionally from the few false social embraces which were worse than a slap in the face. Looking back, I stunned myself at my ability to laugh and joke about any topic, maybe unknowingly wanting the tea party to continue forever, in order not to face life. 'How can it be the end when it is just beginning,' wrote Sophie Large in her book *Sophie's Log*. The beginning of coping without H was looming bleak and stark that evening. You have two choices after all – to live or die yourself.

'How can it be the end when it's just the beginning'

It was roughly at this time I noticed my slowness of speech, that whenever I spoke emotionally speech came slower and slower until grinding to a halt. I like to think it was H's wry humour stopping his generally gung-ho mother making a faux pas, but I suspect in reality it was shock-horror overload. Together with slow speech came foggy exhaustion, and there were mornings when I had to drag my disconnected body out of bed, only wanting to stay cocooned in bedclothes, longing for the end of the day and yet more sleep. Steam-rollered and thrown onto another planet, it was the end of an era – lost son, marriage, home: a changed world. If it had been possible to lock myself in H's room, and throw away the key, I would have been grateful, but this was no longer my home.

Fast forwarding a little, the days crept by with nothing to record but the colour grey pervading everything, interspersed with tennis and dog walking, the tennis organized by a kind and thoughtful friend. Exercise is a must for anyone on emotional overload, and hammering a tennis ball kept my flagging heart and spirit in check. Bottom, my dog, was very ill during this time (chronic arthritis in his off-fore), and I swore often at H for not caring for his much-loved friend. Memories of H swam through this grey fog, but still the tears refused to flow. Even during weekly counselling sessions with my bereavement counsellor Julia Samuel, I held on for grim death, not allowing the pain to seep out – bad for health!

Lottie, now my only remaining offspring, with all the extra pressures that entails, had gone off to New Zealand to continue her interrupted gap year travels. I was doing up H's flat for Lottie's return and I suppose it helped pass the dragging hours. I noticed how increasingly angry I was becoming (not usually a feature among my many faults) and I would descend into Herculean rages over anything and nothing: poor Martin normally the innocent tar-get. Trying to justify myself here, this was in part due to the fact that Harry and he had not seen eye to eye, and my frustration and dis-appointment were erupting. Martin's irritation at H's spiky sensitivity and protectiveness of me, and H's irritation at Martin being around was not a good combination, and I ached for better communication, as I saw H seeking approval: I am sure five years on they would be friends.

At some point during this time, I went to visit the wreckage of H's car; not something I would recommend to the faint hearted, but against all advice I knew it was a must for me. Dumped alongside many other pitiful wrecks, it looked like a grotesque sculpture, the roof spiralling away from the main body held only by a thread of metal, the driver's side heavily scarred, still sprouting chunks of grass and tree bark. The usual bottles of water, notes and maps lit-tered the inside – evidence of H all over – but, luckily, no apparent blood. I listened to the man at the garage explain other tragic stories, as if it was unkind not to include them in their plight along with my son.

Having talked to the policemen who found Harry after his accident, I was loath to let them go, feeling perhaps they were my fading link to Harry, and just getting through the day proved a colossal challenge. Nothing co-operated either physically or mentally, and energy expended in doing the smallest task proved monumental.

The ripples and repercussions of this tragedy continued on and on, my overload forever threatening in the background when tired or under pressure. Although unable to tackle projects in the gung-ho way of old, I was a little encouraged by feeling slightly more patient and tolerant than before (perhaps just too done-in to care).

Now left only with memories and smiling photographs (the former can never be snatched away and the latter serve as testament to his 24 years), the most uplifting moment in any day is hearing his name mentioned or seeing an unexpected photograph. Harry gives me the vital link to connect with people on an emotional level once again, and I am filled with hope that in starting to reconnect with life he will provide the necessary skills as and when he thinks I am ready.

You can't let others in, if all you offer them is a mask

Over five years on, I have become more comfortable in my skin, not worrying about what might happen to me, and have started to do things I might never have contemplated before Harry. It's weird to say life is OK – almost good – yet at the same time carrying within the greatest pain. Harry is ' there', embedded in the souls of all those he loved, living in every breath we take, and mercifully the glimpses of memories that once used to slip just out of reach, feel slightly more stable now. I feel he gives me the vital link to connect with people once more on an emotional level. I don't exactly see his face but feel the warmth of his smile and hear the echo of his voice; he and I laugh together sometimes, and I kiss him, tell him I love him and that I always will ...

Reading my story before it goes to the printers is an uphill struggle, as is reviewing my current status quo. Have I moved on and let go a little? Perhaps. Has there been a tiny corner turned? Maybe. I view clichés like 'moving on' and 'letting go' as either an act of disloyalty or betrayal, or as a sign of no longer caring for my son. Hence my reticence to admit to either.

I know, however, there is a shift in my attitude and approach to life. I talk about my feelings more easily and generally glimpses of my old self appear, hesitantly over the horizon. This means that mega-word 'hope' is dodging and weaving into my life – I hope.

God Gives Us Love, Someone To Love He Lends Us

ALFRED, LORD TENNYSON

Things to help you through the day

Everyone's reactions and feelings after a loss vary both in time and intensity – there is no right or wrong way, so my advice below is not in order of priority, but simply my knee-jerk instinctive thoughts. Please don't think help and recovery comes as a listed package, numbered one to ten. Perhaps my advice below seems glib and all too easy, and I apologize for this, but it is just what helped me.

Whether to see his or her body

You don't have much time to decide this crucial question. CBT are able to give practical and sensitive advice as to the pros and cons, helping you to minimize regrets that may haunt you. I bitterly regret not seeing H; my ex-husband, I suspect was trying to protect me, but as a result I believed for a long time that Harry was decapitated. Just to have seen his feet for identification would have sufficed. In hindsight, personally I feel it is vital to see the body. It's something to do with 'seeing is believing', and therefore, the sooner seen, the sooner believed, even though it is only their 'earthly coat'.

Clothes for the coffin

I suspect the importance of this is more a mother's concern than a father's, but I feel it is very important to decide whether they attend their own funeral in a t-shirt or their Sunday best (another regret of mine). It is a matter of what seems most appropriate.

Friendship/listening/giving time

Seek out your most long-suffering friend as listener to your anguish – your grief is better out than in – but remember even this friend will have limitations and need a rest from time to time. My best friend more or less saved my life and, as a result, those close around me. Try not to be upset with your friend's expectations of your 'grief time' – their lives continue with fresh dramas on the horizon; when they consider you should be 'getting over it' or 'moving on', it is probably only just the beginning of your realization. Life feels so cruel, but to become embittered on top of the isolation you feel won't help – quite the reverse. We are taught how to acquire things, not what to do when we lose them; we have not been 'here' before, so of course we are lost, no maps or signposts. Your friend's time and gift of listening to you is truly precious.

Counselling

Being originally from the 'stiff upper lip' brigade, I was wary of counselling, but five years on I now see it as a lifeline. The trick is to find someone you are comfortable with, and this may take a small amount of research at a time when you are at your most vulnerable. But that hour of feeling safe, away from the world, able to say anything and explore the most random thought is cathartic. You are in the hands of an expert who is trained to help you.

Trying to keep everything together as before

Don't push yourself, trying to be the same person as before – life has changed, will never be the same again. We can only come to terms with this given time, sorting our priorities out and resting our broken brains. If we push, push, push we only exhaust what infinitesimal amount of energy we have.

Music

Listening to music, especially powerful stuff, may make you howl – but so much the better. We seem to have a strange attitude to death in Britain, way more formal than in other countries, where it is acceptable, almost obligatory, to openly wail for days. Starting to feel the pain, acknowledging it in order to edge towards the 'other' side of grieving, is vital for the healing to begin.

Books

It is so reassuring when you feel that there is someone in the same boat as yourself and it is a great comfort when you can empathize with an author. Some books that helped me include:

Sophie's Log – Sophie Large

Conversations with God – Neale Donald Walsch
Grief Recovery Handbook –John W James and Frank Cherry
Rainbows through Clouds – Janet D Glover
Love is letting go of fear – Gerald G Jampolsky
A Grief Observed – CS Lewis
Who said the race is over – Anno Birkin
The Little Prince – Antoine de Saint-Exupery

Anything that helps!

Don't forget, you are on overload – no petrol in the tank – so what's the point of pretending you are OK. I did and it was a big mistake. You are going to need all the help you can get.

Remain open to anything that might help – a girlfriend organized some purple streaks in my hair – it made me smile; perhaps it was Harry's idea as the new Junior Personnel Manager in heaven. Try anything! When feeling like a bull in a china shop and wanting to confront my trauma head-on, or sometimes desperately needing more spiritual help, I tried Rolfing, Reike, mediums, shiatsu, acupuncture, counselling, exercise and keeping a diary. I now paint in watercolour and find it both therapeutic and grounding.

Lastly, wear something of theirs or leave something of theirs around the house. Even though I am left only with a smiling face in a photograph, I would never do without all the photos of H and Lottie in childhood (a nightmare for the person dusting).

Patience within the family

Try to understand the necessity of patience. Eighty-five percent of marriages end in divorce after a loss, partly due to the different ways in which men and women grieve. Keep the communication going so as not to implode your angst and suffering. Remember, if you have children – and even more so if you now have an only child – they are suffering too, feeling guilty, perhaps wondering why it wasn't them that died. The relentless way life moves on when the world should be frozen in sorrow is dire.

Talking to your loved one

This is the best bit – saved until last. Talk to your loved one. It may seem weird, but they say a question asked is always answered; we don't need a chorus line, but just acknowledgement and reassurance that they still are with us. I am continuously asking H's advice and help, and his answers are enough to convince me that it is not me giving the answers I want to hear. Lottie, my daughter was sceptical at first, but now I think she converses with her brother as much as I do. If you want to give this a whirl, be a little patient: sit quietly, preferably on your own to start with, and just ask or speak your thought, either aloud or internally. Then wait. In a short while, you will either hear an answer or feel the response. I promise I am not mad and I have not imagined the many various ways in which I have been helped. Some believe that the dead are truly waiting for them and looking over them. For others it is a matter of holding them in their hearts and mind.

The timing of grief

They say things have to get worse before they get better – perhaps this was written specifically for those grieving. The terrible thing about grief is that for a long time it does get worse. Initially, one is partially anaesthetised by shock, Later when the shock has gone, the savage sadness and pain is even harder to bear. It is over five years later that I can truthfully write that I feel I have turned a tiny corner. Everyone's experience is different as we know, and if I had known this time span at the beginning, I might truly have given up; the only hopeful hint here is – take it hour by hour to start with, and then progress to day by day, setting yourself tiny tasks that can be easily achieved.

There are stages in the grieving process and, irrational as it might seem, those suffering a loss may well experience denial, anger and guilt, before being able to accept that loss. When one has done this, it is necessary to work through the pain of grief, adjust to an environment in which the deceased is missing, and, finally, emotionally relocate the deceased and move on with life.

About A Heartbeat Away

Although I seldon write anything more than a letter, when I do write, I find it marvellously therapeutic, helping to channel my thoughts and thereby address my problems. Giving time to work these thoughts through, then re-reading them, gives a different sense of perspective and leads to clearer thought and purpose. In this sense, I have found writing and compiling *A Heartbeat Away* to be of great personal benefit.

Reading is also a great comfort. Discovering words that aptly describe your own feelings, gives validation and support. In the selections that follow, I hope that you will find something to 'hang your hat on', so to speak. And if you find a modicum of peace and comfort from just one page, I will feel my job has been worthwhile.

The following two poems are examples of bridging feelings with reading and writing. 'A Sparrow Fell' was written by a friend, and it encapsulated for me the rawness and disbelief in understanding the tragedy. Lottie's poem 'When Life is Not the Same' describes feeling like a leper around other people, just like the old 'crossing the street' syndrome.

A Sparrow Fell

From Flappy to God:
A sparrow fell – and no one heard.
Nobody cares. It was just a bird.
From all the numberless flitting throng
Of sparrows, who would miss one song?
But God leaned down and whispered 'I care,
T'was one of my sparrows and I was there'.
Our Harry was killed, full of sunshine and laughter
Full of youthful wild times and some regrets later
And hurts to smooth over, and deeds to applaud
A young man fell; Where were you God?
A young man fell; Why weren't you there?
Is it only for sparrows and such that you care?

If you're God at all – then you could have prevented
This nightmare of pain. So you must have consented.
I've always believed You were loving and good.
I'd like to believe still, if only I could.
But God, if you love me, how can you allow
Such unbearable pain as I'm feeling right now.

Such helplessness – hopelessness – bitter regret,
So many tears that have fallen and yet
So many more that are still locked inside.
Oh God – out there somewhere, have YOU ever cried?
I'm not even sure anymore, that you're real,
But if you are God, do you care how I feel?

From God to Flappy:

Beloved I care. In the midst of your grief,
In the midst of your stricken and crumbling belief,
In the midst of the blackness of total despair,
In the midst of your questioning, child, I am there,
In the midst not far off, in some vague fifth dimension,
But there, where you are, giving you my attention.

My constant attention – and not just today.
Since before you were born, I have loved you this way.
You're important to me, every hair on your head

I have numbered myself. Can these tears that you shed
Go uncounted? Unnoticed? Nay, child, here I stand
Close enough that each teardrop falls into my Hand.

Nor am I a stranger to anguish – to loss
My own Son was taken one day – by a cross.
I know what you suffer. I know what you'll gain,
If you'll let me walk with you into your pain,
I'll carry your grief, and your sorrow I'll bear,
You've only to reach out your hand – I am there.

Let me walk with you now, through the long heavy days;
Let me slowly begin changing heartache to praise.
Take hold of my hand, child, take hold of my love.
I will lead you to joys that you yet know not of.
Your faith may be weak, and your trust incomplete,
But I'll not walk too fast for your stumbling feet.

ANON

When Life is Not the Same

How do people act when they are around me?
It's hard to tell or sense, since I can't see.
I feel a coldness, an uncertainty, a wariness,
Could it have anything to do with my unhappiness?

They're all too frightened to mention to say,
How might I be feeling, or coping today.
I want them to go, no, no I want them to stay,
Can never decide to tell them to go or stay.

How does life continue when life's turned around?
I permanently feel like I've been run aground.
The need to hide and the need to find peace
Is a feeling that I believe will never cease.

Everyone looks and everyone stares,
Not knowing the damaging effect of their glares.
I am changed forever, no doubt about that,
I feel I am forced to wear a 'misery hat'.

You want sympathy one minute, and not the next,
There's no code how to act, nothing written in text,
Is there a formula on how life should or could be,
For one who is grieving, someone like me?

'Cos I know that he's here, all around in the air,
Relishing his fun up in his heavenly lair,
I just wish so hard, that I could get to see him,
But the light up there is faint and painfully dim.

Belief feels shaky, if it is there at all,
I've never really felt His strength or His call,
So who do I turn to now in my hour of need?
For my heart is so heavy and I can't stop the bleed.

I think of you always, in every ounce of my life,
Knowing full well you're there to enjoy both trouble and strife,
Just please stay there through all of my days,
As I need your guidance through my life's long maze.

What I'm trying to say is that I'll love you always,
And that love won't diminish into a misty haze.
I feel your strength every second that I'm here,
And count on the fact that you'll always be near.

LOTTIE SIDEBOTTOM

(WRITTEN IN NEW ZEALAND IN THE IMMEDIATE AFTERMATH OF 5/9/99)

Harry's bear

GRIEF, BEREAVEMENT AND LOSS

Introduction

'If bereavement is a wound, then grief is the inflammation that
   follows.
It causes pain, swelling and disturbance of function.
It can last a long time and may leave scars.
Yet it is the process by which healing occurs.'

RICHARD WILSON

Grief is our unique response to the loss of someone important in
our life. It takes many forms and is one of the most painful experiences that anyone can suffer. Every year thousands of families
experience the tragedy of losing a baby or child, mother or father,
brother or sister, and life is forever changed. Yet through the
process of grieving we can learn how to continue to function and
cope with the future in spite of our losses. Experiencing the pain of
grief is an important part of healing the wound of bereavement.
How well we manage this affects both our quality of life and our
ability to relate to others.

Few people go through life without experiencing the loss of
someone important to them. Death is an inevitable part of life, and
sooner or later we all have to face its harsh reality. Yet death is so
often a taboo subject. With improved health care, our expectations
are that we, and those who are important in our lives, will live until

old age. How painful it is, then, to suffer the death of a child or for children to experience the death of a parent. Such deaths are out of the natural order of things as we expect them to happen. The grief in these situations is a natural reaction, but to an abnormal event, and can be very much harder to manage. The family is never whole again.

Grief can be very isolating. Relatives and friends, in their desire not to intrude, and also in self-protection, may think it is best to say nothing and sidestep the issue. Many bereaved people are frequently ignored by others and quickly learn that to hide their feelings is more acceptable in society and that it reduces the discomfort of others. However, it is acknowledging the significance of the loss and finding ways of accepting the reality that helps the bereaved to express their painful feelings and allows them to grieve for the person who has died.

Grief is not a mental illness, although anxiety, fear, anger and a preoccupation with self can all add up to a feeling of 'going mad'. These feelings are natural and when experienced and expressed will become less frequent and begin to subside over time. Talking about them together as a couple and bringing them into the open can be helpful. Expressing grief is cathartic and attempts to short-circuit these feelings rarely help in the long term and may cause deep-seated problems in the years ahead. If grief is denied, not spoken about, or anger, guilt and depression persist to the exclusion of other feelings, bereavement counselling support as a couple can be helpful.

A mother's response to the loss of a child is frequently different to that of a father's. To illustrate the difference Margaret Stroebel (et al; 1993) proposed a dual model of grieving in which people engage in both loss-oriented and restoration-oriented grieving activity and oscillate between the two behaviours. Women naturally tend to be loss-oriented and are usually more concerned with their feelings. They focus on their loss, their child and the emotions they are experiencing. They want and need memories to help them constantly recall and be reminded of their child who has died.

In contrast, men are often more restoration-oriented. They want and need things to return to normal as soon as possible. Traditionally men are not encouraged to have feelings and so they instinctively may try to suppress them and endeavour to be strong, as society demands, and may even function as if nothing had happened. This response may be misinterpreted by their partner as not caring about their child.

When people engage in either activity to the exclusion of the other, it can cause added difficulties. Women may need to help develop some form of restorative response to enable them to move on from the intensity of the pain of loss and men may need to be helped to allow themselves to explore their painful feelings.

These different ways of dealing with grief can put a significant strain on the parents' relationship. It is helpful for them to understand that their partner's response to grief is natural and to find ways of sharing their feelings and reach out to one another.

Grieving is an essential and necessarily painful healing process. It means feeling and expressing all the emotions you have. It also means slowly accepting the reality of what has happened and learning to live with the change that has taken place in your life.

Facing life without someone you love is difficult and painful. No one can fill the aching void, and each day can bring constant reminders of their absence. Just getting through the day can seem an insurmountable task. The future may seem uncertain or even frightening. One of the most difficult aspects of grieving is the feeling of being out of control. Grief is a solitary, messy, exhausting and relentless business, but it is survivable. As human beings, we have infinite resources within ourselves to heal and move forward, if only we first allow ourselves the time to express the pain.

Reinvesting in the future involves letting go of the person who has died and moving on in life without them. This can feel like a betrayal, yet moving on is not about forgetting, but about finding ways to remember that person and finding a permanent place for them in your life, where it does not cause you so much pain.

Grieving is different for everyone. There are no rules to follow. In grief, we do as we must. The most important thing is to understand that your grief is natural and is your way of expressing how you feel. Speaking about the person who has died, remembering them and all they meant to us, doing things that are meaningful and connected with them is, for many, as necessary as eating and sleeping. It is neither helpful nor appropriate to compare or judge the intensity of feelings involved in grief. Everyone is different, and one person's grief may be as painful as another's, regardless of the circumstances. So often, it is our previous experiences of loss and grief that affect the way we feel about our current loss.

We each must grieve in our own way, at our own pace. Time alone does not heal – it is only through grieving that we begin to work through the pain of loss. When someone dies, our feelings for them and memories of them stay alive and active inside us. We need to find ways of expressing those feelings so that we can move on in our lives. Our memories are their parting gifts to us.

Ann Chalmers
Chief Executive

Jenni Thomas OBE
President

If I can stop one Heart from breaking
I shall not live in vain
If I can ease one Life the aching
Or cool one pain.
Or help one fainting Robin
Unto his nest again
I shall not live in vain.

EMILY DICKINSON

On Pain

Your pain is the breaking of the shell that encloses your understanding.
Even as the stone of the fruit must break, that its heart may stand
in the sun, so must you know pain.
And could you keep your heart in wonder at the daily miracles
of your life, you pain would not seem less wondrous than
your joy;
And you would accept the seasons of your heart, even as you have
always accepted the seasons that pass over your fields.
And you would watch with serenity through the winters of your
grief.

KAHIL GIBRAN

Grief cannot be shared, for it is mine alone.
Grief is a dying within me.
a great emptiness,
a frightening void.
It is a loneliness,
a sickening sorrow at night,
on awakening a terrible dread.
Another's words do not help.
A reasoned argument explains little
for having tried too much.
Silence is the best response to another's grief.
Not the silence that is a pause in speech,
awkward and unwanted,
But one that unites heart to heart.

CARDINAL BASIL HUME

May I try to tell you again where your only comfort lies? It is not in the forgetting the happy past. People bring us well-meant but miserable consolations when they tell us what time will do to help our grief. We do not want to lose our grief, because our grief is bound up with our love and we could not cease to mourn without being robbed of our affections.

PHILLIPS BROOKS

For those still left to die

For those still left to die
For those we love
who pass on through;
all the coloured mixture,
poignancy and love.

But we're alone, still left to mourn.
We're left behind, still left to die.
In bitter pain we bash the rock.
We eat to live,
We live to cry

I look for heaven in soaking fields
of crashing downpour, dark and wet.
In morbid skies and moaning seas,
I find their face;

and then it's gone.

And all my analogies lead me to lonely sadness.

And in the fire of bitter frustration,
my jagged anger screams its rage
of burning tears.
The anger of 'Why?', and the pain of 'Goodbye',
never said.

Behind every silver lining, a grey cloud.
Replace the sun with cold bereavement.
Is there a heaven or is there hell?

But with all this pain it stays inside.
I don't express it.
I don't dare to express it.

JAMES MADDOX

When we lose a friend we die a little

ANON

Sometimes when one person is missing, the whole world seems
depopulated.

ALPHONSE DE LAMARTINE

The Lesson

'Your father's gone', my bald headmaster said.
His shiny dome and brown tobacco jar
Splintered at once in tears. It wasn't grief.
I cried for knowledge which was betterer
Than any grief. For there and then I knew
That grief has uses – that a father dead
Could bind a bully's fist a week or two;
And then I cried for shame, then for relief.

I was a month past ten when I learnt this:
I still remember how the noise was stilled
In school-assembly when my grief came in,
Some goldfish in a bowl quietly sculled
Around their shining prison on its shelf.
They were indifferent. All the other eyes
Were turned towards me. Somewhere in myself
Pride, like a goldfish, flashed a sudden fin.

EDWARD LUCIE-SMITH

For children

Fleetingly known, yet ever remembered.
These are our children now and always:
These whom we see not, we will forget not,
Morning and evening all of our days.

Lives that touched our lives, tenderly, briefly,
Now in the one light living always:
Named in our hearts now, safe from all harm now,
We will remember all of our days.

As we recall them, silently name them,
Open our hearts, Lord, now and always:
Grant to us, grieving, love for the living:
Strength for each other all of our days

Safe in your peace, Lord, hold these our children;
Grace, light, and laughter grant them each day:
Cherish and hold them till we may know them
When to your glory we find our way.

CHRISTINE ROSSETTI

Epitaph on a Child

Here, freed from pain, secure from misery, lies
A child, the darling of his parents' eyes:
A gentler Lamb ne'er sported on the plain,
A fairer flower will never bloom again:
Few were the days allotted to his breath;
Now let him sleep in peace his night of death.

THOMAS GRAY

'Then, said Mr. Valiant-for-Truth, I am going to my Father's; and though with great difficulty I am got hither, yet now I do not repent me of all the trouble I have been at to arrive where I am. My sword I give to him that shall succeed me in my pilgrimage, and my courage and skill to him that can get it. My marks and scars I carry with me, to be a witness for me, that I have fought his battles who will now be my rewarder. When the day that he must go hence was come, many accompanied him to the riverside, into which as he went he said, Death, where is thy sting? And as he went down deeper, he said, Grave, where is thy victory? So he passed over, and all the trumpets sounded for him on the other side.'

JOHN BUNYAN, FROM *THE PILGRIM'S PROGRESS*

As you love me, let there be no mourning when I go. Rather of your sweet courtesy rejoice with me at my soul's release from captivity.

SIR WALTER RALEIGH

Everyday tragedies

We do not expect people to be deeply moved by what is not unusual. The element of tragedy which lies in the very fact of frequency has not yet wrought itself into the coarse emotion of mankind; and perhaps our frames could hardly bear much of it. If we had a vision and feeling of all ordinary human life, it would be like hearing the grass grow and the squirrel's heartbeat, and we should die of that roar which lies on the other side of silence.

GEORGE ELIOT

Not how did he die?
But how did he live?
Not what did he gain?
But what did he give?
These are the units to measure the worth
Of this man as a man, regardless of birth.
Not what was his station?
But had he a heart?
How did he play his God-given part?
Was he at hand with a word of good cheer
To bring back a smile or banish a fear?
Not what was his church or what was his creed?
But had he befriended those really in need?
Not how did the formal obituary run?
But how many grieved when his life's work was done?

ANON

Death is the transition
from a regular state of consciousness
into a higher collective state
To die is to become one with the universe.

***

Smile now,
I am gone.
Don't hold on
for too long.
The rope'll slip away.

***

I saw from this place at the foot of my grave I
gave myself in awe to childish hope and promise.
The tomb it was dug by those whom you know and love
    and trust.
There's just room enough to put you in.
And you fear that you lust and you know what you love must
    be clean.
And you fear what you've seen, what you've touched, what
    you've been.
And I'm touched.
I'm not naming anyone at all.

I'm soon to return, there's soon to be fire in my veins again.
I'm almost home.
I'm almost ready.

ANNO BIRKIN

The Epitaph

Here rests his head upon the lap of Earth
A Youth to Fortune and to Fame unknown.
Fair Science frowned not on his humble birth,
And Melancholy marked him for her own.

Large was his bounty, and his soul sincere,
Heaven did a recompense as largely send:
He gave to Mis'ry all he had, a tear,
He gained from Heaven ['twas all he wished] a friend.

No further seek his merits to disclose,
Or draw his frailties from their dread abode,
[There they alike in trembling hope repose]
The bosom of his Father and his God.

THOMAS GRAY, (FROM 'ELEGY WRITTEN IN A COUNTRY CHURCHYARD')

When he shall die,
Take him and cut him out in little stars
And he will make the face of heaven so fine
That all the world will be in love with the night
And pay no worship to the garish sun.

WILLIAM SHAKESPEARE

And death shall have no dominion.
Dead men naked they shall be one
With the man in the wind and the west moon;
When their bones are picked clean and the clean bones gone,
They shall have stars at elbow and foot;
Though they go mad they shall be sane,
Though they sink through the sea they shall rise again;
Though lovers be lost love shall not.
And death shall have no dominion.

And death shall have no dominion.
Under the windings of the sea
They lying long shall not die windily;
Twisting on racks when sinews give way,
Strapped to a wheel, yet they shall not break;

Faith in their hands shall snap in two,
And the unicorn evils run them through;
Split all ends up they shan't crack;
And death shall have no dominion.

And death shall have no dominion.
No more may gulls cry at their ears
Or waves break loud on the seashores;
Where blew a flower may a flower no more
Lift its head to the blows of the rain;
Though they be mad and dead as nails
Heads of the characters hammer through daisies;
Break in the sun till the sun breaks down,
And death shall have no dominion.

DYLAN THOMAS

High Flight

Oh, I have slipped the surly bonds of earth,
And danced the skies on laughter-silvered wings;
Sunward I've climbed and joined the tumbling mirth
Of sun-split clouds – and done a hundred things
You have not dreamed of; wheeled and soared and swung
High in the sun-lit silence. Hovering there
I've chased the shouting wind along, and flung
My eager craft through footless halls of air;
Up, up the long, delirious, burning blue
I've topped the wind-swept heights with easy grace,
Where never lark not even eagle flew;
And while, with silent lifting mind I've trod
The high untrespassed sanctity of space,
Put out my hand, and touched the face of God.

JOHN GILLESPIE MAGEE

The death of a young person affects us at a deep almost primeval level. We react with gut-wrenching horror to disasters which kill children and to child murders, and if we are so deeply moved how does anyone cope with the death of their own child?

Children are our future, they are the tangible symbols of the immortality of the human race and, for parents, of their own immortality in their children and in their children's children. In the modern western world we do not expect to have to bury our own children. It's the natural order of creation gone awry. Children are deeply vulnerable. When a child dies the parents feel they have failed in the most fundamental responsibility of all – that of protecting their child.

***

'Losing a child is the opposite of giving birth to it. When you have a child you create bonds of love between you. When that child dies you have to undo those bonds in order to let go. I have four children, two here and two in another place. The two that are not here are very much with me, in the seasons, in the wind, the sun, the rain, the stars, in other children. They are just everywhere, unfettered by physical restrictions.'

FROM GOOD HOUSEKEEPING, 1993

I suppose it is that human relationships are what give meaning and heart to our life, and when we lose a beloved person, some of the meaning is taken out of life and the future looks less rich. That is the point at which I am beginning to see that here, when we have got that space hollowed out within us, the comforting love of God can come towards us and it's something beyond our comprehension. It's something coming towards us from God to fill the emptiness, and God is the ultimate meaning in life, and sometimes we have to have a sense of meaninglessness before we can really discover that it is God who is at the centre ...

It doesn't have to be just loss of a person. It can be all kinds of loss – loss of place, loss of a particular job. All these things can show us something of our mortality and cause us to look beyond.

It's often only as we experience something painful in our lives that our hearts become broken open, and as they become broken open we become more sensitive to the pain of others and to the pain of the world.

SISTER CAROL, FROM *FINDING YOUR STORY*

A farewell is necessary before you can meet again.

RICHARD BACH FROM *ILLUSIONS*

Then Almitra spoke, saying, We would ask now of Death.

And he said:

You would know the secret of death.

But how shall you find it unless you seek it in the heart of life?

The owl whose night-bound eyes are blind unto the day cannot unveil the mystery of light.

If you would indeed behold the spirit of death, open your heart wide unto the body of life. For life and death are one, even as the river and the sea are one.

In the depth of your hopes and desires lies your silent knowledge of the beyond;

And like seeds dreaming beneath the snow your heart dreams of spring.

Trust the dreams for in them is hidden the gate to eternity.

Your fear of death is but the trembling of the shepherd when he stands before the king whose hand is to be laid upon him in honour.

Is the shepherd not joyful beneath his trembling, that he shall wear the mark of the king/

Yet is he not more mindful of his trembling?

For what is it to die but to stand naked in the wind and to melt into the sun?

And what is it to cease breathing but to free the breath from the restless tides, that it may rise and expand and seek God unencumbered?

Only when you drink from the river of silence shall you indeed sing.

And when you have reached the mountain top, then you shall begin to climb.

And when the earth shall claim your limbs, then shall you truly dance.

KAHIL GIBRAN, *THE PROPHET*

Cowards

Cowards die many times before their deaths:
The valiant never taste of death but once
Of all the wonders that I have yet heard,
It seems to me most strange that men should fear;
Seeing that death, a necessary end,
Will come, when it will come.

WILLIAM SHAKESPEARE, *JULIUS CAESAR* (11:11)

But time flies meanwhile, flies never to return.

VIRGIL, *GEORGICS*, 11

To everything there is a season, and a time to every purpose under the heaven: a time to be born and a time to die; a time to plant, and a time to pluck up that which is planted; a time to kill, and a time to heal; a time to break down, and a time to build up; a time to weep and a time to laugh; a time to mourn, and a time to dance; a time to cast away stones, and a time to gather stones together; a time to embrace, and a time to refrain from embracing; a time to seek, and a time to lose; a time to keep, and a time to cast away; a time to rend, and a time to sew; a time to keep silence, and a time to speak; a time to love, and a time to hate; a time for war, and a time for peace.

ECCLESIASTES 3:1–8

In memoriam

I sometimes hold it half a sin
To put in words the grief I feel:
For words, like Nature, half reveal
And half conceal the Soul within.

But, for the unquiet heart and brain,
A use in measured language lies;
The sad mechanic exercise,
Like dull narcotics, numbing pain.

In words, like weeds, I'll wrap me o'er,
Like coarsest clothes against the cold;
But that large grief which these enfold
Is given in outline and no more.

ALFRED, LORD TENNYSON

No one ever told me that grief felt so like fear. I am not afraid, but the sensation is like being afraid. The same fluttering in the stomach, the same restlessness, the yawning. I keep on swallowing.

At other times it feels like being mildly drunk, or concussed. There is a sort of invisible blanket between the world and me. I find it hard to take in what anyone says. Or perhaps, hard to want to take it in. It is so uninteresting. Yet I want the others to be about me. I dread the moments when the house is empty. If only they would talk to one another and not to me.

CS LEWIS, FROM *A GRIEF OBSERVED*

All is well

Death is nothing at all. I have only slipped away into the next room. I am I and you are you. Whatever we were to each other that we are still. Call me by my old familiar name, speak to me in the easy way which you always used. Put no difference in your tone; wear no forced air of solemnity or sorrow. Laugh as we always laughed at the little jokes we enjoyed together. Play, smile, think of me, pray for me. Let my name be ever the household word that it always was. Let it be spoken without effort, without the ghost of a shadow on it. Life means all that it ever meant. It is the same as it ever was: there is absolutely unbroken continuity. Why should I be out of mind because I am out of sight? I am waiting for you at an interval, somewhere very near, just around the corner, All is well.

HENRY SCOTT HOLLAND

Remember

Remember me when I am gone away,
Gone far away into the silent land;
When you can no more hold me by the hand,
Nor I half turn to go yet turning stay.
Remember me when no more day by day
You tell me of our future that you planned:
Only remember me; you understand
It will be late to counsel then or pray.

Yet if you should forget me for a while
And afterwards remember, do not grieve:
For if the darkness and corruption leave
A vestige of the thoughts that once I had,
Better by far you should forget and smile
Than that you should remember and be sad.

CHRISTINA ROSSETTI

For I am persuaded that neither death,
Nor life, nor angels, nor principalities,
Nor powers, nor things present,
Nor things to come,
Nor height, nor depth, nor any other creature,
Shall be able to separate us from the love of God
Which is in Christ Jesus our Lord.

ROMANS 8:38

Then a woman said, Speak to us of Joy and Sorrow.

And he answered:

Your joy is your sorrow unmasked.
And the selfsame well from which your laughter rises was often-times filled with your tears. And how else can it be?
The deeper that sorrow carves into your being, the more joy you can contain.
Is not the cup that holds your wine the very cup that was burned in the potter's oven?
And is not the lute that soothes your spirit the very wood that was hollowed by knives?
When you are joyous, look deep into your heart and you shall find it is only that which has given you sorrow that is now giving you joy.
When you are sorrowful, look again in your heart and you shall see that in truth you are weeping for that which has been your delight.

Some of you say 'Joy is greater than sorrow', and others say, 'Nay, sorrow is the greater.' But I say to you they are inseparable.
Together they come, and when one sits alone with you at your board,
Remember that the other is asleep on your bed.

Verily you are suspended like scales between your sorrow and your joy.
Only when you are empty are you at standstill and balanced.
When the treasure keeper lifts you to weigh his gold and silver,
Needs must your joy or your sorrow rise or fall.

KAHIL GIBRAN, *THE PROPHET*

Farewell my Friends

It was beautiful, as long as it lasted
The journey of my life.
I have no regrets whatsoever
Save the pain I'll leave behind.
Those dear hearts who love and care.
And the strings pulling at the heart and soul.

The strong arms that held me up
When my own strength let me down.
At every turning of my life
I came across good friends
Friends who stood by me
Even when the time raced me by.

Farewell, farewell my friends
I smile and bid you goodbye.
No shed no tears for I need them not
All I need is your smile.

If you feel sad do think of me
For that's what I'll like
When you live in the hearts of those you love
Remember then, you never die.

RABINDRANATH TAGORE

If I should die

If I should die, and leave you
Be not like others, quick undone
Who keep long vigil by the silent
Dust and weep.

For my sake turn to life and smile
Nerving thy heart and trembling hand
To comfort weaker souls than thee.
Complete these unfinished tasks of mine
And I perchance may therein comfort thee.

THOMAS GRAY

A new normal

The pain never goes away. It is there with you every second that you breathe, every step that you take. Gradually it softens and becomes a part of your life, a part of who you are, a part of the relationship between you and your child. In time this new life seems so normal and it is normal. Normal to cry, normal to feel sad, normal to be thinking of your child all the time; normal for him not to be in your life. You may hate how it makes you feel but you cannot change anything and so you get on with life and carry your pain through each day.

Sometimes it is unbearable, eating away at the foundations of the new life you have fought so hard to build. It tears apart the strength you have wrapped around your broken dreams and exposes the damage you have suffered since your child died.

As bereaved parents we are expected to leave our child in the past, to 'move on' or 'let go'. It is why we feel so isolated from society, from family and friends. We are expected to take this child, whose attachment to us was not severed with the umbilical cord and pack him away like old, out-dated clothes. A child we had nurtured and loved every second our lives touched, whose connection with us was on every level of our existence, a child who filled our world with the miracle of his smile.

We so not have to 'leave' our child. We can move forward into a new life and take our child with us. Every time we think of our child they are a part of that moment. I know that we cannot see our child by our side, we cannot hold them, but the love we felt for each other is embedded in our soul, runs through our veins and inhabits every breath we take.

***

I have a life. A life rising gradually from the destruction of your leaving. I am trying to build on ground that shakes, on beliefs that can be torn away on a whim. It is so difficult to make progress when life has shown that there is no permanence. You plan your future only to see your dreams lying shattered, you look at the remains of your world and know that it has ended. You have no choice but to rebuild but with what? Everything is broken, pieces no longer fit and where once you were complete there is an immense hole. You are bewildered, lost, you search but cannot find yourself. You have forgotten who you are, You ask 'Am I dead too?' and the answer is yes.

You are now small and blank – an open book waiting for that first imprint. You are surrounded by devastation. You have a choice: to sit amongst the damage, asking why, making no attempt to salvage what you once loved or to slowly stand, regain your balance, and, gathering your broken world together begin to construct a new life.

From a torn pattern, held together with love, you begin again. Just when you believe your foundations are solid, they crack and you are, once again, damaged. Each time the destruction lessens and your strength grows.

SUE WHITE

They who speak to me do not know that my heart is full with your unspoken words.

They who crowd in my path do not know that I am walking alone with you.

They who love me do not know that their love brings you to my heart.

They who are near me do not know that you are nearer to me than they are.

RABINDRANATH TAGORE

Watercolour painting of Harry's rose by Flappy Lane Fox. In the summer of 1999, Harry spent a hot day cutting a swathe through the jungle in the walled garden, seemingly with only weeds surrounding him. Three months after his death that September, at exactly the spot where he had sat at lunch that day, a rose appeared in full bloom.

Watercolour painting of a French hamlet by Flappy Lane Fox. She was painting this scene when she received the news of Harry's accident. It is unfinished.

Watercolour painting by Charlie Mackesy. Harry's favourite picture.

An etching by Harry, aged 11. He was engraving the etching with the Longridges when their studio nearly caught fire, due to turpentine rags catching fire.

Though I am dead grieve not for me with tears
Think not of death with sorrowing and fears
I am so near that every tear you shed
Touches and tortures me, though you think me dead.
But when you laugh and sing in glad delight
My soul is lifted upward to the light.
Laugh and be glad, for all that life is giving
And I, though dead, will share your joy of living.

ANON

An odd by-product of my loss is that I'm aware of being an embarrassment to everyone I meet. At work, at the club, in the street, I see
people, as they approach me, trying to make up their minds
whether they'll 'say something about it' or not. I hate it if they do,
and if they don't. Some funk it altogether. R has been avoiding me
for a week. I like best the well-brought-up young men, almost boys,
who walk up to me as if I were a dentist, turn very red, get it over,
and then edge away to the bar as quickly as they decently can. Perhaps the bereaved ought to be isolated in special settlements like
lepers. To some I'm worse than an embarrassment. I am a death's
head. Whenever I meet an happily married pair I can feel them both
thinking, 'One or the other of us must some day be as he is now.'

CS LEWIS, FROM *A GRIEF OBSERVED*

Do not stand at my grave and weep
I am not there, I do not sleep.
I am a thousand winds that blow
I am the softly falling snow,
I am the gentle rains that fall
I am the fields of grain,
I am in the morning lush
I am in the graceful rush
Of beautiful birds in circling flight.
I am the starshine of the night
I am in the flowers that bloom
I am in a quiet room.
I am in the birds that sing,
I am in each lovely thing.
Do not stand at my grave and cry
I did not die.

MARY ELIZABETH FRYE

Unspoken

Dear Friend: Please put it behind you;
let it go for a while.
You're too lost in mourning;
lighten up, try to smile.
I know it's a tragedy.
I know how you must feel,
but you must just get through it,
move on so you'll heal.

I just can't stand
to see you in pain.
I know if you try
you'll be happy again.

Dear Friend: The person you still
want me to be
is gone, locked away,
and I don't have the key.
I'm really not choosing
to be like this,
but my life is pure feeling,
clenching me like a fist.
There's a bleak somber moat
between me and the world,
the drawbridge so heavy,
splintered edges so cruel.
When I venture out strongly,
the pain wraps me still,
colours my actions,
saps at my will.
So please don't give up,
though I'm hopeless and lost.
Our friendship's true value
reflects in its costs.

GENESSE BOURDEAU GENTRY

You see the world through eyes that are blind to my life. You do no walk in my shoes and yet you believe that you would take different steps. While you feel happiness I have forgotten what it feels like, while you live with hope mine has been crushed.

You look at me and still see someone you have always known. That is what you want to see. All I ask of you is that you listen to me. I cannot be that person anymore, cannot pretend that I see life as you do. The innocence in my life has been destroyed, the belief in my future lies broken and buried with my son. For me there is only this moment. I have lost the excitement you feel as you anticipate your plans, your happiness as they come to fruition. My joys in life are fleeting, shallow glimpses – a moment's pleasure in the sun on my face; a child's smile; the beauty in a butterfly poised for flight. Like my child they do not stay for long.

You are so quick to tell me how you think I should feel. Do you live in my nightmare? Do you share my pain? Do you miss my son? You should not judge me while you walk on soft sand and I walk on shards of glass, should not expect me to think as you do when I am not you.

I carry my burden on thin ice. Often it breaks and I struggle but your patience is exhausted and I must cling to the edge alone until I am stronger. You have turned your back on me just when my need is greatest. I do now judge you when you turn away for you measure grief by your own experience, but grief is immeasureable. You tell me that you cannot imagine my pain and yet expect me to experience emotions beyond my grasp.

Am I selfish when you ask me to be happy or are you?

***

No matter how much time passes, I still cannot believe that you have gone forever.

I know it, but knowing and believing are not the same. My mind lives in reality; it awakens each morning knowing you are not in your bedroom; it knows you will not kiss my cheek and say 'see you later' as you used to; it knows you will not smile at me as you leave. My mind knows the pain that awaits as I open my bedroom door each morning to look upon the world I must now inhabit without you; that along with the clothes I put on each day I must wear an extra layer to become the person others see.

Belief lives alongside reality but it lies in my heart and my heart cannot cope with forever. This moment is all it will allow me, all I can have. I cannot contemplate a future without you so I let life happen minute by minute. Your death taught me that I may not always have another minute.

You look out at me from photographs and although I know you once lived in my world, I wonder if you ever existed. I know that once your hand touched mine; that your laughter once filled our house; that you always made me smile but I cannot feel my memories.

I have so many wonderful memories but they are no substitute for you and only leave me feeling cheated. They do not take away my pain, I do not believe anything ever will.

SUE WHITE

God's Lent Child

'I'll lend you for a little while, a child of mine' God said.
'For you to live while he lives, and mourn for when he's dead.
He may be six or seven years, or forty-two or three,
But will you till I call him back, take care of him for me?
He'll bring his charms to gladden you, and should his stay
     be brief
You'll always have his memories as a solace in your grief
I cannot promise he will stay, for all from earth return
But there are lessons taught below I want this child to learn.
I've looked this whole world over in my search for teachers true
And from the folk that crowd Life's lane, I have chosen you
Now will you give him all your love and not think the labour vain,
Nor hate me when I come to take this lent child back again.
I fancy that I heard them say 'Dear God, Thy will be done',
For all the joys this child will bring, the risk of grief we'll run.
We will shield him with tenderness, we'll love him while we may.
And for all the happiness we've known, we'll ever grateful stay.
But should the angels call him much sooner than we'd planned
We'll brave the bitter grief that comes and try to understand.'

ANON

I think you are only as happy as your unhappiest child.

CAROLINE SNOW

And what of fear, of waiting and not knowing what a sunrise will see?

In that darkness, what is possible overwhelms what is probable and the coldness of uncertainty grows even colder in its own anxious weather.

CHEYENNE WOMAN

From the beach, the child, holding the hand of her father,
Those burial-clouds that lower, victorious, soon to devour all,
Watching, silently weeps.

Weep not, child,
Weep not, my darling,
With these kisses let me remove your tears;
The ravening clouds shall not long be victorious,
They shall not long possess the sky – shall devour the stars only in
    apparition:
Jupiter shall emerge – be patient – watch again another night – the
    Pleiades shall emerge,
They are immortal – all those stars, both silvery and golden, shall
    shine out again,
The great stars and the little ones shall shine out again – they
    endure;
The vast immortal suns, and the long-enduring pensive moons,
    shall again shine.

WALT WHITMAN, FROM 'ON THE BEACH AT NIGHT'

In troubled water you can scarce see your face or see it very little, till the water be quiet and stand still. So in troubled times you can see little truth; when times are quiet and settled truth appears.

JOHN SELDEN

The body shuts down when it has too much to bear, goes its own way quietly inside waiting for a better time, leaving you numb and half alive.

JEANETTE WINTERSON, FROM 'PASSION'

They shall grow not old as they that are left grow old,
Age shall not weary them, nor the years condemn;
At the going down of the sun and in the morning
We shall remember them.

LAURENCE BINYON

I walked a mile with Pleasure;
She chatted all the way,
But left me none the wiser
For all she had to say.

I walked a mile with Sorrow
Ad ne'er a word said she;
But oh, the things I learned from Her
When Sorrow walked with me!

ROBERT BROWNING

God grant me the serenity to accept the things I can't change,
courage to change the things I can, and the wisdom to know the
difference.

SERENITY PRAYER

The Soldier

If I should die, think only this of me:
That there's some corner of a foreign field
That is for ever England. There shall be
In that rich earth a richer dust concealed;
A dust whom, England bore, shaped, made aware,
Gave, once, her flowers to love, her ways to roam,
A body of England's breathing English air,
Washed by the rivers, blessed by suns of home.

And think, this heart, all evil shed away,
A pulse in the eternal mind, no less
Gives somewhere back the thoughts by England given;
Her sights and sounds; dreams happy as her day;
And laughter, learnt of friends; and gentleness,
In hearts at peace, under an English heaven.

RUPERT BROOKE

Because I could not stop for death

Because I could not stop for Death –
He kindly stopped for me –
The carriage held but just ourselves –
And Immortality.

We slowly drove – He knew no haste
And I had put away
My labor and my leisure too,
For his civility –

We passed the school, where children strove
At recess – in the ring –
We passed the fields of gazing grain –
We passed the setting sun

Or rather – He passed us –
The dews drew quivering and chill –
For only gossamer, my gown –
My tippet – only tulle –

We paused before a house that seemed
A swelling of the ground –
The roof was scarcely visible –
The cornice – in the ground –

Since then – 'tis centuries – and yet
Feels shorter than the day
I first surmised the horses' heads
Were toward Eternity –

EMILY DICKENSON

'His sun went down while it was still day.'

JEREMIAH 15:9

Do not go gentle into that good night

Do not go gentle into that good night,
Old age should burn and rave at close of day;
Rage, rage against the dying of the light.

Though wise men at their end know dark is right
Because their words had forked no lightning they
Do not go gentle into that good night.

Good men, the last wave by, crying how bright
Their frail deeds might have danced in a green bay,
Rage, rage against the dying of the light.

Wild men who caught and sang the sun in flight,
And learn, too late, they grieved it on its way
Do not go gently into that good night.

Grave men near death, who see with blinding sight
Blind eyes could blaze like meteors and be gay,
Rage, rage against the dying of the light.

And you, my father, there on the sad height,
Curse, bless, me now with your fierce tears, I pray.
Do not go gentle into that good night.
Rage, rage against the dying of the light.

DYLAN THOMAS

Death is the future for everyone. It is the last post of this life and the reveille of the next. Death is the end of our present life, it is the parting from loved ones, it is setting out into the unknown. We overcome death by accepting it as the will of a loving God, by finding Him in it.

Death, like birth, is only a transformation, another birth. When we may die we shall change our state, that is all.

In faith in God, it is as easy and natural as going to sleep and waking up there.

POPE JOHN XXIII, FROM *JOURNAL OF A SOUL*

Because I have loved life, I shall have no sorrow to die.
I have sent up my gladness on wings, to be lost in the blue of
  the sky.
I have run and leapt with the rain, I have taken the wind to my
  breast.
My cheek like a drowsy child to the face of the earth I have
  pressed.
Because I have loved life, I shall have no sorrow to die.

I have kissed young Love on the lips, I have heard his song to
  the end.
I have struck my hand like a seal in the loyal hand of a friend.
I have known the peace of heaven, the comfort of work done well.
I have longed for death in the darkness and risen alive out of hell.
Because I have loved life, I shall have no sorrow to die.

I give a share of my soul to the world where my course is run.
I know that another shall finish the task I must leave undone.
I know that no flower, nor flint was in vain on the path I trod.
As one looks on a face through a window through life I have
  looked on God.
Because I have loved life, I shall have no sorrow to die.

AMELIA JOSEPHINE BURR

If we shall live, we live

If we shall die; we die:
If we live we shall meet again:
But tonight, goodbye.
One word, let but one be heard –
What, not one word?

If we sleep we shall wake again
And see tomorrow's light:
If we wake, we shall meet again:
But tonight, goodnight
Goodnight, my lost and found –
Still not a sound?

If we live, we must part;
If we die, we part in pain:
If we die, we shall part
Only to meet again.
By those tears on either cheek,
Tomorrow you will speak.

To meet, worth living for:
Worth dying for, to meet,
To meet, worth parting for:
Bitter forgot in sweet.
To meet, worth parting before
Never to part more.

CHRISTINA ROSSETTI

From too much love of living,
From hope and fear set free,
We thank with brief thanksgiving
Whatever gods may be
That no life lives forever;
That dead men rise up never;
That even the weariest river
Winds somewhere safe to sea.

ALGERNON CHARLES SWINBURNE

Blue Mountains to the north of the walls.
White winding river about them;
Here we must make separation
And go through a thousand miles of dead grass.
Mind like a floating wide cloud,
Sunset like the parting of old acquaintances
Who bow over their clasped hands at a distance.
Our horses neigh to each other
As we are departing.

EZRA POUND

HOPE,
HUMOUR
AND LOVE

INTRODUCTION

Linford Cazenove and Harry Sidebottom died in car accidents within a week of each other. Flappy and I had never met but a mutual friend was able to introduce us almost immediately after our sons' funerals. We became very close, very quickly and have been a great support to each other since. Together we 'had to accept the unacceptable' as my dear friend Alan Bates, who had also lost a son, Tristan told me at the time. A loved one's mortality, especially your child's, is harder to bear than your own.

Our darling sons died five years ago now – we will never 'get over it' but I think that Linford and Harry must be proud of our (albeit slow!) progress. I have learned through Linford's death that love, compassion and a desire to help those in need, live in the hearts of most human beings. The kindness and understanding that was shown to us in our despair was limitless – and, extraordinarily, from many people who had never met us. This led me to believe that these qualities live naturally in the hearts of most human beings. More recently, we have all born witness to the support of every kind, that the nations of the world have given to the victim countries of the tsunami in December 2004. We all know that death is something to be endured eventually – there is little evidence to suggest that it can be avoided! But the fact that another's mortality can be harder to bear than our own and I think that is an exhilarating testament to the real meaning of what it is to be human.

ANGHARAD REES

***

I agree with all Angharad has said and would only add that the seemingly unendurable pain does ease with time, especially if one can somehow set one's mind on the joy our lost love ones gave to us and their friends. Whether or not one believes in an afterlife or, indeed, in a God, there is no doubting that Linford's spirit continues to influence not just his immediate family, but the lives of all who knew him.

I think it is very important to keep up a dialogue with our loved one's friends – Angharad and I find great solace and joy in having a party each year on the anniversary of Linford's death to celebrate what was given to us rather than mourn what was taken away.

CHRISTOPHER CAZENOVE

Look you, the stars shine still.

JOHN WEBSTER (FROM *THE DUCHESS OF MALFI*)

I'd thought that time would stop if you had died
That sun and moon and stars would disappear
That earth itself might vanish into darkness
If I had lost a life I held so dear.

But though you're gone the sun still heralds the day
And darkness only brings a brief respite
The world goes on, and those who never knew you
Just cannot know the grief that's in my heart.

Yet even in that grief I keep the gladness
That comes from having loved you and been loved
And even in my anguish and my sorrow
Somehow your presence seems to ease my aching heart.

I see your smile and share still in your laughter
I talk to you and feel that you are near
I know that somehow you can still be with me
To help me bear the grief that's ever here.

I so believe that love can live for ever
That happiness of memory conquers pain
And though the world seems empty now without you
I know that sometime we will meet again.

ANON

Life goes on

If I should go before the rest of you
Break not a flower nor inscribe a stone,
Nor when I'm gone speak in a Sunday voice
But be the usual selves that I have known.
Weep if you must, parting is hell
But life goes on, so sing as well.

JOYCE GRENFELL

'In one of the stars I shall be living. In one of them I shall be Laughing. And so it will be as if all the stars were laughing when you look at the stars at night …

And when your sorrow is comforted, [time soothes all sorrows] you will be content that you have known me. You will always be my friend. You will want to laugh with me …

And your friends will be properly astonished to see you laughing as you look up at the sky! … That night I did not see him set out on his way. He got away from me without making a sound'.

ANTOINE DE SAINT-EXUPÉRY, FROM *THE LITTLE PRINCE*

The Clock of Life

The clock of life is wound but once,
And no man has the power
To tell just when the hands will stop
At late or early hour.

To lose one's wealth is sad indeed,
To lose one's health is more,
To lose one's soul is such a loss
That no man can restore.

The present only is our own,
So Live, Love, toil with a will –
Place no faith in 'Tomorrow' –
For the clock may then be still.

ROBERT H SMITH

Without your wealth a little lost
Without your health a lot is lost
Without your friends all is lost.

MAJOR GERALD ASHTON GUNDRY

Live your life

Live you life that the fear of death
can never enter your heart.
Trouble no one about his religion,
respect others in their views
and demand that they respect yours.
Love your life, perfect your life,
beautify all things in your life.
Seek to make your life long
and of service to your people.
Prepare a noble death song for the day
when you go over the great divide.
Always give a word or sign of salute when meeting
or passing a friend, or even a stranger, if in a lonely place.
Show respect to all people but grovel to none.
When you rise in the morning, give thanks fro the light,
for your life, for your strength.
Give thanks for your food and for the joy of living.
If you see no reason to give thanks,
the fault lies in yourself.
Touch not the poisonous firewater that makes wise ones turn
    into fools
and robs the spirit of its vision.
When your time comes to die, be not like those
whose hearts are filled with fear of death,
so that when their time comes they weep and pray
for a little more time to live their lives over again
in a different way.
Sing your death song, and die like a hero going home.

CHIEF TECUMSEH OF THE SHAWNEE NATION

Always with you

Your mother is always with you.
She's the whisper of the leaves
as you walk down the street.
She's the smell of bleach
in your freshly laundered socks.
She's the cool hand on your brow
When you're not well.
Your mother lives inside your laughter.
She's crystallized in every teardrop.
She's the place you came from,
your first home.
She's the map you follow
with every step you take.
She's your first love
and your first heartbreak ...
and nothing on earth can separate you.

ANON

A Strong Woman

A strong woman works out every day
to keep her body in shape ...
but a woman of strength
kneels in prayer to keep her soul in shape ...

A strong woman isn't afraid of anything ...
but a woman of strength
shows courage in the midst of her fear ...

A strong woman won't let anyone
get the best of her ...
but a woman of strength
gives the best of herself to everyone ...

A strong woman makes mistakes
and avoids the same in the future ...
but a woman of strength
realizes life's mistakes can also be God's
blessings and capitalizes on them ...

A strong woman walks sure footedly ...
but a woman of strength
knows God will catch her when she falls ...

A strong woman wears the look of
confidence on her face ...
but a woman of strength wears grace ...

A strong woman has faith that
she is strong enough for the journey ...
but a woman of strength has faith
that it is in the journey that she will become strong ...

ANON

The Presence of Love

And in Life's noisiest hour,
There whispers still the ceaseless love of thee
The heart's self-solace and soliloquy.

You mould my hopes, you fashion me within;
And to the leading love-throb in the heart
Thro' all my being all my pulses beat.
You lie in all my many thoughts, like light
Like the fair light of dawn, or summer eve
On rippling stream or cloud-reflecting lake.

And looking to the heaven, that bends above you
How oft I bless the Lot that made me love you.

SAMUEL TAYLOR COLERIDGE

Love is to have you in my heart and hold you there forever,
Through all chance and earthly changes.

ROBERT BROWNING

Footprints in the Sand

One night I dreamed I was walking along the beach with the Lord. Many scenes from my life flashed across the sky. In each scene I noticed footprints in the sand. Sometimes there were two sets of footprints, other times there was one only.

This bothered me because I noticed that during the low periods of my life, when I was suffering from anguish, sorrow or defeat, I could see only one set of footprints, so I said to the Lord,

'You promised me Lord, that if I followed you, you would walk with me always. But I have noticed that during the most trying periods of my life there has only been one set of footprints in the sand. Why, when I needed you most, have you not been there for me?'

The Lord replied, 'The years when you have seen only one set of footprints, my child, is when I carried you.'

MARY STEVENSON

It is often said that something may survive of a person after his death, if that person was an artist and put a little of himself into his work. It is perhaps in the same way that a sort of cutting taken from one person and grafted on to the heart of another continues to carry on its existence even when the person from whom it had been detached has perished.

MARCEL PROUST, FROM *REMEMBRANCE OF THINGS PAST*

A smile costs nothing, but gives much.

It enriches those who receive,

without making poorer those who give.

It takes but a moment,

but the memory of it sometimes lasts forever.

None is so rich or mighty that he can get along without it,

and none is so poor but that he can be made rich by it.

A smile creates happiness in the home,

fosters good will in business,

and is the countersign of friendship.

It brings rest to the weary,

cheer to the discouraged,

sunshine to the sad,

and it is nature's best antidote for trouble.

Yet it cannot be bought, begged, borrowed, or stolen,

for it is something that is of no value to anyone

until it is given away.

Some people are too tired to give you a smile.

Give them one of yours,

as no one needs a smile so much

as he who has no more to give.

(ATTRIB. RABBI SAMSON RAPHAEL HIRSCH)

Up-hill

Does the road wind up-hill all the way?
Yes, to the very end.
Will the day's journey take the whole long day?
From morn to night, my friend.

But is there for the night a resting-place?
A roof for when the slow dark hours begin.
May not the darkness hide it from my face?
You cannot miss that inn.

Shall I meet other wayfarers at night?
Those who have gone before.
Then must I knock, or call when just in sight?
They will not keep you standing at that door.

Shall I find comfort, travel-sore and weak?
Of labour you shall find the sum.
Will there be beds for me and all who seek?
Yea, beds for all who come.

CHRISTINA ROSSETTI

No funeral gloom, my dears, when I am gone.
Corpse-gazings, tears, black raiment, graveyard grimness,
Think of me withdrawn into the dimness,
Yours still, you mine.
Remember all the best of our past moments
and forget the rest.
And so to where I wait, come gently on.

ELLEN TERRY

Look to this day

Look to this day! For it is life, the very life of life.
In its brief course lie all the varieties and realities of your
    existence;
the bliss of growth, the glory of the action, the splendour
    of beauty.
For yesterday is already a dream, and tomorrow is only a vision,
but today, well lived, makes every yesterday a dream of happiness,
and every tomorrow a vision of hope. Look well, therefore, to
    this day!
Such is the salutation of the dawn.

SANSKRIT PROVERB

Fytte 8

Life is mostly froth and bubble,
Two things stand like stone,
Kindness in another's trouble,
Courage in your own.

ADAM LINDSAY GORDON, FROM *YE WEARIE WAYFARER*

To love someone deeply gives you strength,
Being loved by someone deeply gives you courage.

LAO TZU

It isn't for the moment you are struck that you need courage. But
for the long uphill climb back to sanity and faith and security.

ANNE MORROW LINDBERGH

The life that I have is all that I have
And the life that I have is yours
The love that I have of the life that I have
Is yours and yours and yours.

A sleep I shall have, a rest I shall have
And death will be but a pause
For the years I shall have in the long green grass
Are yours and yours and yours.

LEO MARKS

A Sensitive Plant in a garden grew,
And the young winds fed it with silver dew,
And it opened its fan-like leaves to the light.
And closed them beneath the kisses of Night.

And the Spring arose on the garden fair,
Like the Spirit of Love felt everywhere;
And each flower and herb on Earth's dark breast
Rose from the dreams of its wintry rest.

PERCY BYSSHE SHELLEY, FROM 'THE SENSITIVE PLANT'

How Can I Keep from Singing

My life flows on in endless song
Above earth's lamentation.
I hear the real though far-off hymn
That hails a new creation.
No storm can shake my inmost calm
While to that rock I'm clinging
It sounds an echo in my soul,
How can I keep from singing?

I lift my eyes, the cloud grows thin;
I see the blue above it;
And day by day this pathway smooths,
Since first I learned to love it.
The peace of Christ makes fresh my heart,
A fountain ever springing;
All things are mine since I am his,
How can I keep from singing?

ROBERT LOWRY

So She May Hear

Hillside walk
above the sea,
memories, songs,
wash over me.

Every breath
and every thought,
there is no place
where she is not.

Bright sun, blue sky,
so crisp and clear.
I sing my songs,
so she may hear.

GENESSE BOURDEAU GENTRY

For everything exists and not
one sigh nor smile nor tear,
one hair nor particle of
dust, not one can pass away.

WILLIAM BLAKE

Never give up, no matter what is going on,
Never give up.
Develop the heart – too much energy is spent these days in
developing the mind instead of the heart.
Be compassionate – not just to your friends, but to everyone.
Be compassionate,
Work for peace in your heart and in the world.
Work for peace and, I say again,
Never give up.
No matter what is happening,
No matter what is going on around you
Never give up.

HIS HOLINESS THE 14TH DALAI LAMA

Katrina's Sun-Dial

Hours fly,
Flowers die:
New days,
New ways:
Pass by!
Love stays.

HENRY VAN DYKE

Don't let fear frighten you into doing nothing.
Don't become so paralysed by fear that you can't
respond in any given situation. Don't be so
frightened of being frightened that you don't take
on anything difficult, for fear of failure.

RICHARD LINDLEY

Time Is

Time is too Slow for those who Wait,
Too Swift for those who Fear,
Too Long for those who Grieve,
Too Short for those who Rejoice;
But for those who Love,
Time is not.

HENRY VAN DYKE

See everything
Overlook a lot
Correct a little

POPE JOHN XIII

Be the person your dog thinks you are.

ANON

He who binds to himself a joy
Does the winged life destroy;
But he who kisses the joy as it flies
Lives in eternity's sun rise.

WILLIAM BLAKE

I thank Thee, God, that I have lived
In this great world and known its many joys;
The song of the birds, the strong, sweet scent of hay
And cooling breezes in the secret dusk,
The flaming sunsets at the close of day,
Hills, and the lonely, heather-covered moors,
Music at night, and moonlight on the seas,
The beat of waves upon the rocky shore
And wild, white spray, flung high in ecstasy:
The faithful eyes of dogs, and treasured books,
The love of kin and fellowship of friends,
And all that makes life dear and beautiful.

I thank Thee, too, that there has come to me
A little sorrow and, sometimes, defeat,
That comes with parting, and the words, 'Goodbye,'
Dawn breaking after dreary hours of pain,
When I discovered that night's gloom must yield
And morning light breaks through to me again.
Because of these and other blessings poured
Unasked upon my wondering head,
Because I know that there is yet to come
An even richer and more glorious life,
And most of all, because Thine only Son
Once sacrificed life's loveliness for me –
I thank Thee, God, that I have lived.

ELIZABETH CRAVEN

When I am dead, my dearest,
Sing no sad songs for me;
Plant thou no roses at my head,
Nor shady cypress tree:
Be the green grass above me
With showers, and dewdrops wet;
And if thou wilt, remember,
And if thou wilt, forget.

I shall not see the shadows,
I shall not feel the rain;
I shall not hear the nightingale
Sing on, as if in pain:
And dreaming through the twilight
That doth no rise nor set,
Haply I may remember,
And haply may forget.

CHRISTINA ROSSETTI

Your children are not your children.
They are the sons and daughters of Life's longing for itself.
They come through you but not from you,
And though they are with you yet they belong not to you.
You may give them your love but not your thoughts,
For they have their own thoughts.

You may house their bodies but not their souls,
For their souls dwell in the house of tomorrow, which you
cannot visit, not even in your dreams.
You may strive to be like them, but seek not to make them
    like you.
For life goes not backward nor tarries with yesterday.

KAHIL GIBRAN, *THE PROPHET*

Yesterday is the past
Tomorrow is the future
Today is a gift
That's why we call it the present.
One life
One chance
Make it count
You deserve happiness.

ANON

If you love something, set it free. If it comes back to you, it's yours. If it doesn't, it never was. We do not possess anything in this world, least of all other people. We only imagine that we do. Our friends, our lovers, our spouses, even our children are not ours; they belong only to themselves. Possessive and controlling friendships and relationships can be as harmful as neglect.

ALISON WILLCOCKS

To laugh often and love much, to win the respect of intelligent persons and the affection of children; to earn the approbation of honest critics and endure the betrayal of false friends; to appreciate beauty; to find the best in others; to give one's self; to leave the world a bit better, whether by a healthy child, a garden patch or a redeemed social condition; to have played and laughed with enthusiasm and sung with exultation: to know even one life has breathed easier because you have lived, this is to have succeeded.

***

God grant me serenity to accept the things I cannot change; the courage to change the things I can; and the wisdom to know the difference.

RALPH WALDO EMERSON

A smile costs nothing, but gives much.
It enriches those who receive,
without making poorer those who give.
It takes but a moment,
but the memory of it sometimes lasts forever.
None is so rich or mighty that he can get along without it,
and none is so poor but that he can be made rich by it.
A smile creates happiness in the home,
fosters goodwill in business,
and is the countersign of friendship.
It brings rest to the weary,
cheer to the discouraged,
sunshine to the sad,
and it is nature's best antidote for trouble.
Yet it cannot be bought, begged, borrowed, or stolen,
for it is something that is of no value to anyone
until it is given away.
Some people are too tired to give you a smile.
Give them one of yours,
as no one needs a smile so much
as he who has no more to give.

ANON

I long to take your load,
I want to bear your burdens too
But this you must remember
This one thing you must know,
I cannot take your burden
Until you let it go.

SELKIRK BAPTIST PRAYER

Why Not Ask Me?

I hear it again and again,
one friend asked another how I have been.
How hard, really, would it be
to pick up the phone and just ask me?

GENESSE BOURDEAU GENTRY

Do not let us fear things too much, for we
often suffer more from the things we fear
than from those which really come to
pass. Rejoice to think that after having
recovered yourself in the midst of interior
pain and difficulty, you will be able to help others
in their turn. No one can help except
he who has suffered.

ABBE DE TOURVILLE

Pied a terre?
A pied a terre?
That may well be what the dead
Call our earthly life.

ANNE BLOCH

I stand upon a sea shore, a ship spreads her white sails to the morning breeze, and heads across the blue ocean. She is an object of beauty and strength, and I stand and watch her until at length she hangs like a speck of white cloud on the horizon just where the sea and the sky meet to mingle with each other. At my side someone says, 'There! She's gone.'

Gone where? Gone from my sight – that is all. She is just as large in mast and spar and hull as when we sailed close by, and just as able to bear her living freight to the place of destination. Her diminished size is in my vision alone. At the moment when someone says 'There! She's gone,' other eyes watching her coming and other voices take up the shout, 'Here she comes!' And that is dying.

BISHOP BRENT

Happiness is like a butterfly. The more you chase it, the more it eludes you. Then you turn your mind to other things and it comes and sits silently on your shoulder.

HENRY DAVID THOREAU

You can't live on hope, but it should be on the menu.

ANON

May the promise of springtime, cheer you
And the magic that it brings, thrill you;
May the healing of the sunlight warm you
And the blessings of God fill you.

May the peace of the flowing waters, calm you,
And the strength of the hills uphold you;
May the joy of waking earth, enrich you,
And the blessings of St Michael enfold you.

May the music of the morning, lift you,
And the hope of all the world, guide you;
May the love of those you love, sustain you,
And the blessings of St Peter stay beside you.

ANON

Happy the man, and happy he alone,
He who can call today his own;
He who, secure within, can say,
Tomorrow do thy worst, for I have lived today.
Be fair or foul or rain or shine
The joys I have possessed, in spite of fate, are mine.
Not Heaven itself upon the past has power,
But what has been, has been, and I have had my hour.

JOHN DRYDEN

Everyone Sang

Everyone suddenly burst out singing;
And I was filled with such delight
As prisoned birds must find in freedom,
Winging wildly across the white
Orchards and dark-green fields; on – on – and out of sight.

Everyone's voice was suddenly lifted;
And beauty came like the setting sun;
My heart was shaken with tears; and horror
Drifted away ... O, but everyone
Was a bird; and the song was wordless; the singing will
 never be done.

SIEGFRIED SASSOON

Announcement in The Cork Examiner

Donnachie's Bar, Cork. Due to the sad death of Paddy, the bar to all
intents and purposes, will remain closed during our grief: but so as
not to inconvenience our esteemed customers, the door will remain
ajar. 'Tis what Paddy wanted. Thank you.

THE DONNACHIE FAMILY

Suffering and Wonder

Her death left a firestorm of destruction
and desolation in its wake –
ashes, our lives blackened, twisted stumps,
burnt free of superfluity,
dead to life, to joy, full of
smoke and shadow-covered dreams.

'Suffering is the base of happiness' Thich Nhat Hanh says,
'You can learn from your suffering. And then
you have a chance to be happy. But if you don't
know anything about suffering, I don't think
happiness can be real and deep.'

Today I am happy; I know that I have suffered,
and I will suffer more because of my daughter's death.
That layering of suffering and grief is boundless,
both nourishing me and holding me back. At times
I succumb to its heavy weight, making me feel lethargic –
the slow creep of molasses in my mind and body,
the downward drag of her death instead of
the upward flying wonder of her life.

At other times, like now, I know that I am healing,
that new shoots are coming up through blackened ground
and that from dead-looking stumps is sprouting new life.
I feel the nourishing, budding aspect
that suffering and grief have brought to open me
to parts of myself unknown to me ever before her death.

In these times, I know her presence as so much more
in spirit than ever could have been in life. Though I
long to touch and hold her with my physical being,
I instead hold her with my heart and mind and feel
the new growth poke through the tear-filled soil
and find that it is mixed with angel's dust.

GENESSE BOURDEAU GENTRY

I wish you enough sun to keep your attitude bright.
I wish you enough rain to appreciate the sun more.
I wish you enough happiness to keep your spirit alive.
I wish you enough pain so that the smallest joys in life appear
    much bigger.
I wish you enough gain to satisfy your wanting.
I wish you enough loss to appreciate all that you possess.
I wish enough 'Hello's' to get you through the final 'Goodbye.

BOB PERKS

And a youth said, Speak to us of friendship.

And he answered, saying:

Your friend is your needs answered. He is your field which you sow with love and reap with thanksgiving. And he is your board and your fireside. For you come to him with your hunger, and you seek him for peace.

When your friend speaks his mind you fear not the 'nay' in your own mind, nor do you withhold the 'ay'. And when he is silent your heart ceases not to listen to his heart; for without words, in friendship, all thoughts, all desires, all expectations are born and shared, with joy that is unacclaimed.

When you part from your friend, you grieve not; for that which you love most in him may be clearer in his absence, as the mountain to the climber is clearer from the plain. And let there be no purpose in friendship save the deepening of the spirit. For love that seeks aught but the disclosure of its own mystery is not love but a net cast forth: and only the unprofitable is caught.

And let your best be for your friend. If he must know the ebb of your tide, let him know its food also. For what is your friend that you should seek him with hours to kill? Seek him always with hours to live. For it is his to fill your need, but not your emptiness. And in the sweetness of friendship let there be laughter, and sharing of pleasures. For in the dew of little things the heart finds its morning and is refreshed.

KAHIL GIBRAN, *THE PROPHET*

May the road rise with you.
May the wind be always at your back,
May the sun shine warm upon your face
And the rain fall soft upon your fields:
And until we meet again,
May God hold you in the hollow of his hand.

OLD IRISH BLESSING

Deep peace of the running wave to you.
Deep peace of the flowing air to you.
Deep peace of the quiet earth to you.
Deep peace of the shining stars to you.
Deep peace of the infinite peace to you.

CELTIC PRAYER

BEREAVEMENT SUPPORT
ORGANISATIONS

British Association for Counselling & Psychotherapy
1 Regent Place, Rugby
Warwickshire CV21 2PJ

Tel: 0870 4435252
E-mail: bacp@bacp.co.uk
Website: www.counselling.co.uk

Childhood Bereavement Network
8 Wakeley Street
London EC1V 7QE

Tel: 020 7843 6309
Website: www.ncb.org.uk/cbn

Cruse-Bereavement Care
Cruse House, 126 Sheen Road
Richmond, Surrey TW9 1UR

Tel (Office): 020 8940 4818
Helpline: 0870 167 1677

E-mail: info@crusebereavementcare.org.uk
Website: www.crusebereavementcare.org.uk

SANDS (Stillbirth & Neonatal Death Society)
28 Portland Place
London, W1B 1LY

Tel: 020 7436 7940
Helpline: 020 7436 5881
Website: www.uk-sands.org
E-mail: support@uk-sands.org

The Child Bereavement Trust
Aston House, High Street
West Wycombe, High Wycombe
Bucks. HP14 3AG

Tel: 01494 446648
E-mail: enquiries@childbereavement.org.uk
Information and Support Line: 0845 357 1000 (This valuable
service was established through funds raised in memory of Harry
Sidebottom).
Website: www.childbereavement.org.uk

The CBT provides specialized training for professionals to
improve their response to the needs of grieving families, and produces resources and information for children and families, and all
the professionals who come into contact with them in the course of
their work. The ethos of learning from bereaved families underpins
all of the Charity's work.

The Compassionate Friends
53 North Street
Bristol BS3 1EN

Tel (Office): 0117 966 5202
Helpline: 0117 953 9639
E-mail: mailto:info@tcf.org.uk
Website: www.tcf.org.uk

ACKNOWLEDGEMENTS

Heartfelt thanks to Lottie, for her love and support; Martin, for surviving my hell and still being here; Martin's grandchildren for showing me the joy of new life; Mel for her wisdom; Julia Samuel – an inspiration; Monica Jonsson – a magician; Caroline Meindl for mending my broken pieces; Elizabeth Muszka for her care; all my friends for their loyalty; the Reverend Hugh Maddox, a wonderful listener; The Child Bereavement Trust for showing me the way forward; Ann-Marie Evans for also showing me the way forward; Angharad Rees for her companionship in grief; and to my dog Jambo – a perfectly timed present from Harry. Thanks also to Hatty Lane Fox for her advice, editor Matthew Cory for his unstinting expertise, Jo Ridgeway for her design, and Monica Green for her help with the production of this book, Carole Tonkinson for her guidance, and Charlie Mackesy for his generosity and support. Thanks to Robbie Williams for 'Angel' and Katie Melua for 'The Closest Thing to Crazy' which both touched a chord.

PERMISSIONS

Grateful acknowledgment is given for permission use the works as follows:

Edward Lucie-Smith, 'The Lesson', (*Changing Shape: New and Selected Poems*, Carcanet Press, 2002); Joyce Grenfell, 'Life Goes On', (in Daisy Goodwin, 101 Poems to Get You Through the Day ..., HarperCollins, 2000); Dylan Thomas, 'And Death Shall Have No Dominion' and 'Do Not Go Gentle Into That Good Night', (*Collected Poems: 1934–1953*, JM Dent, 1988); Jeanette Winterson for an extract from *The Passion* (Penguin, 1988); Elena Gaussen Marks for Leo Mark's poem 'The Life That I Have'; Richard Lindley for his poem 'Don't Let Fear Frighten You', and Alison Willcocks, 'If You Love Something' (from *Seize the Day*, Albery Wienrich et al (ed), Chatto and Windus, 2001); George Sassoon for Siegfried Sassoon's poem 'Everyone Sang' (*Collected Poems 1908–1956*, Faber, 1984); Genesse Bourdeau Gentry for her poems 'Unspoken', 'So She May Hear', 'Why Not Ask Me?' and 'Suffering and Wonder' from *Stars in the Deepest Night*, (Writer's Club Press, 1999): 'Why Not Ask Me?' also appeared in the publication *The Compassionate Friends* (TCP).

While every reasonable effort has been made to seek the permission of the copyright holders whose work has been quoted in this book, the publishers would be interested to hear from any copyright holders whose permission has not been obtained.

111